Benchmark and Unit Tests

Grade 1

Photo Credits

Cover (t) Key (t) right; (b) left; (c) center; (l) top; (c) bottom; (bg) background
(tl) ©Comstock; (t) ©George Doyle/Stockbyte/Getty Images/HMH Corbis.

Copyright © by Houghton Mifflin Harcourt Publishing Company

Printed in the U.S.A.

ISBN 978-0-547-87158-5

10   0928   21 20 19 18 17 16 15 14

4500 000000   A B C D E F G

 HOUGHTON MIFFLIN HARCOURT

Contents

Contents

Name _____ Date _____

Reading and Analyzing Text

Read the story "Pam Looks for a Friend" before answering Numbers 1 through 8.

Pam Looks for a Friend

Pam is sad.

Pam can not play.

Pam does not have a friend here.

What can Pam do?

Pam can look for a friend.

A tan cat runs to Pam.

It is Tom.

Pam pets Tom.

A big dog runs to Pam.

It is Sam.

Pam pets Sam.

To the teacher: Read the directions and questions with children. Selection and answer choices should be read independently.

Name _____ Date _____

Pam looks at Tom and Sam.

Can Tom play?

Can Sam play?

Yes! They can play.

Tom and Sam play tag with Pam.

Pam has many friends here.

Pam is not sad.

Now answer Numbers 1 through 8. Base your answers on the story "Pam Looks for a Friend."

1 How does Pam feel at the START of the story?

○ big

○ mad

○ sad

2 Read this sentence from the story.

Pam does not have a friend here.

What does the word *friend* mean in the sentence above?

○ good

○ like

○ pal

3 Read this sentence from the story.

Pam can look for a friend.

What does the word *look* mean in the
sentence above?

○ funny

○ go find

○ like to play

4 What happens BEFORE a big dog runs
to Pam?

○ Pam pets Tom.

○ Pam looks at Sam.

○ Tom and Sam play.

5 Read this sentence from the story.

Pam pets Sam.

Which word means almost the SAME as the
word *pets* in the sentence above?

○ has

○ pats

○ sits

Name _____ Date _____

6 What happens AFTER Pam pets Sam?

○ Pam looks for a friend.

○ Pam looks at Tom and Sam.

○ Sam looks for Pam and Tom.

7 Read this sentence from the story.

Tom and Sam play tag with Pam.

What picture shows what the word *tag* means
in the sentence above?

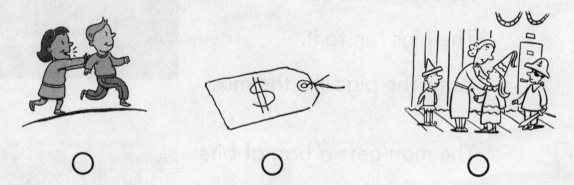

○   ○   ○

8 How does Pam feel at the END of the story?

○ not sad

○ not good

○ a bit mad

Name _____ Date _____

Read the article "Many Jobs" before answering Numbers 9 through 15.

Many Jobs

The sun is up.

The man is up, too.

The man gets a mix.

He sets it in a tub.

The pigs run to it.

Yum! The pigs like the mix.

The man gets a bag of bits.

He tips the bag.

The hens run to get the bits.

Yum! The hens like the bits.

Read Together To the teacher: Read the directions and questions with children. Selection and answer choices should be read independently.

Name _____ Date _____

The man gets a can.

He pops up the lid.

The cat runs to the man.

Yum! The cat likes it.

The man can not sit yet.

He has many jobs to do.

Now answer Numbers 9 through 15. Base your answers on the article "Many Jobs."

9 Read this sentence from the article.

He sets it in a tub.

Which picture shows what the word *he* means in the sentence above?

○   ○   ○

10 How do you know this article is real?

○ The pigs say, "Yum!".

○ The hens play with food.

○ The photos show live things.

11 What does the SECOND photo show?

   ○ what is in the tub

   ○ what the pigs look like

   ○ what the hens look like

12 Read this sentence from the article.

The cat runs to the man.

Which word is an action word in the
sentence above?

   ○ The

   ○ cat

   ○ runs

13 Read these sentences from the article.

Yum! The cat likes it.

Why does the author use the word *yum*?

   ○ to show the cat is happy

   ○ to show the cat is thirsty

   ○ to show the cat is sleepy

9

14 Read this sentence from the article.

He has many jobs to do.

What is the meaning of the word *many* in the sentence above?

○ help

○ lots

○ sing

15 What is the MAIN idea of this article?

○ The man is up.

○ The pigs like the cat.

○ The man has many jobs.

STOP

Name _____ Date _____

Phonics

Answer Numbers 16 through 25. Choose the best answer for each question.

16 Which word BEST completes the sentence below?

Look at the _____.

○ cat

○ cot

○ cut

17 Which word BEST completes the sentence below?

Cat has a _____.

○ wag

○ web

○ wig

18 Which word BEST completes the sentence below?

_____ **is funny.**

○ At

○ In

○ It

19 Which word BEST completes the sentence below?

The _____ plays, too.

○ fax

○ fix

○ fox

20 Which word BEST completes the sentence below?

He _____ for the cat.

○ has

○ hop

○ hops

Name _____ Date _____

21 Which word BEST completes the sentence below?

The cat _____ hop with his pal.

○ can

○ cot

○ cub

22 Which word BEST completes the sentence below?

They have _____.

○ fan

○ fin

○ fun

23 Which word BEST completes the sentence below?

The cat and fox are _____.

○ hat

○ hot

○ hut

24 Which word BEST completes the sentence below?

What can the fox _____?

○ get

○ got

○ gut

25 Which word BEST completes the sentence below?

The fox finds a _____.

○ fan

○ fin

○ fun

Writing to Narrate

Read the prompt and plan your response.

> Most people have a fun friend.
>
> Think about a friend you have who is fun.
>
> Draw a picture of your friend having fun.
>
> Then write a label for your picture.

Planning Page

Use this space to make notes before you start writing. The writing on this page will **NOT** be scored.

_____

- -

_____

_____

- -

_____

Read Together To the teacher: Read this page with children. Have them plan their writing on this page. Then have them draw their picture in the box on the following page. Direct them to write a label for the picture on the lines below it.

Name _____ Date _____

Start your response here. The writing on this page WILL be scored.

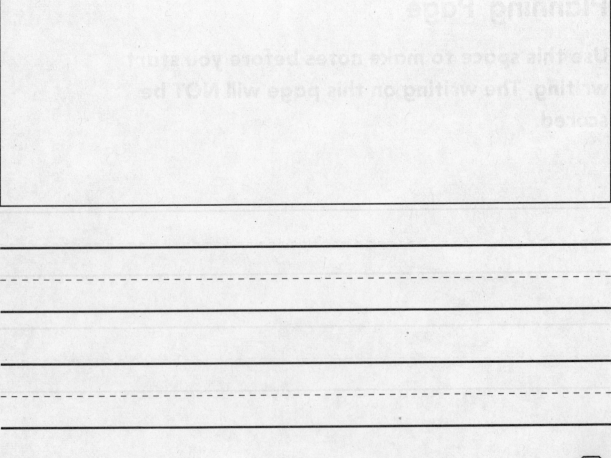

16

Name _____ Date _____

Reading and Analyzing Text

Read the story "Friends" before answering Numbers 1 through 8.

Friends

Miss Stock let the class eat a snack.

Jan got her box.

She will eat plums.

Kim did not pack a snack today.

Jan can help.

Jan will give Kim a plum.

Jan is a good friend.

17

Name _____ Date _____

Miss Stock let the class draw.

Kim got her pens.

She will draw pictures.

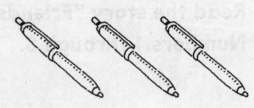

Jan did not pack pens today.

Kim can help.

Kim will give Jan some pens.

Now Kim is a good friend.

Kim and Jan are glad to be friends.

18

Name _____ Date _____

Now answer Numbers 1 through 8. Base your answers on the story "Friends."

1 Where does the story take place?

2 Read this sentence from the story.

Miss Stock let the class eat a snack.

Which picture shows what the word *eat* means
in the sentence above?

○   ○   ○

Name _____ Date _____

3 Read this sentence from the story.

Jan will give Kim a plum.

What is a *plum*?

○ a kind of box

○ a kind of pen

○ a thing to eat

4 Why does Jan give Kim a plum?

○ Kim does not have a snack.

○ Jan does not like to eat plums.

○ Miss Stock asks Jan to give a plum to Kim.

5 Read this sentence from the story.

Miss Stock let the class draw.

Which picture shows what the word *draw* means in the

sentence above?

6 Read this sentence from the story.

Jan did not pack pens today.

Which word means almost the SAME as the word *pack* in the sentence above?

○ bring

○ buy

○ get

7 Read the chart below.

| Kim got her pens to draw pictures. | → | Jan did not pack pens today. | → | |

Which sentence BEST completes the chart?

○ Kim gets a box.

○ Kim has some plums.

○ Kim lets Jan have some pens.

8 Which sentence BEST tells about Kim?

○ She helps.

○ She has lots of plums.

○ She does not like to draw.

Name _____ Date _____

Read the article "How to Look After a Cat" before answering Numbers 9 through 15.

How to Look After a Cat

My animal is a cat.

It is fun to have a pet.

You have lots of jobs!

Here are some jobs you must do.

A cat has to eat.

Put small bits in a pan.

A cat has to sip.

Fill a pan for the cat.

A cat has to play.

Let it jump and run after you.

A cat has to nap.

Make a soft bed.

A cat would like a friend.

Give it a pat.

Do every job here.

You will have a glad cat!

Now answer Numbers 9 through 15. Base your answers on the article "How to Look After a Cat."

9 What does the title tell you the article will be about?

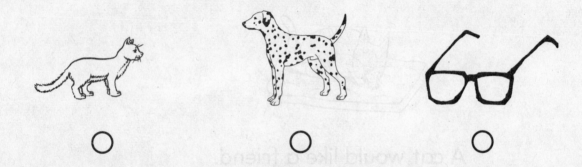

○   ○   ○

10 Read this sentence from the article.

My animal is a cat.

Which picture shows another *animal*?

○   ○   ○

11 Read this sentence from the article.

You have lots of jobs!

Which word means almost the SAME as the word *lots* in the sentence above?

○ like

○ many

○ one

12 Read this sentence from the article.

Put small bits in a pan.

Which word has the OPPOSITE meaning of the word *small*?

○ big

○ fast

○ help

13 What does the FIRST picture show?

○ what the cat eats

○ why the cat plays

○ how the cat helps

14 Which job helps the cat take a nap?

○ Give it a pat.

○ Make a soft bed.

○ Fill a pan for the cat.

15 Why is it good to pat a cat?

○ A cat has to eat.

○ A cat has to nap.

○ A cat would like a friend.

Name _____ Date _____

Phonics

Answer Numbers 16 through 25. Choose the best answer for each question.

16 Which word BEST completes the sentence below?

Rick and Sam _____ what to put in the bag.

○ black

○ plan

○ plant

17 Which word BEST completes the sentence below?

They get to take a _____.

○ clip

○ drip

○ trip

 Read Together To the teacher: Read the directions and questions with children. Target sentences and answer choices should be read independently.

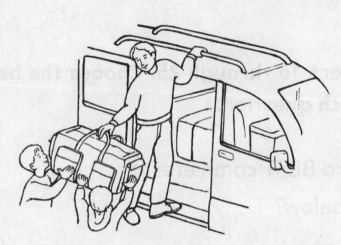

18 Which word BEST completes the sentence below?

Dad puts the bags in the _____ of the van.

○ back

○ ball

○ bats

19 Which word BEST completes the sentence below?

Some bags _____ not fit.

○ add

○ miss

○ will

20 Which word BEST completes the sentence below?

Rick and Sam help Dad _____ up the bags.

○ lift

○ milk

○ pond

21 Which word BEST completes the sentence below?

They help Dad _____ the bags on top of the van.

○ scrap

○ stack

○ swam

22 Which word BEST completes the sentence below?

Dad gets a _____ to hold the bags to the top of the van.

- ○ scamp
- ○ strap
- ○ struck

23 Which word BEST completes the sentence below?

The bags will not _____ off the van now.

- ○ brag
- ○ crop
- ○ drop

Name _____ Date _____

24 Which word BEST completes the
sentence below?

Rick and Sam look at the _____.

○ clock

○ flap

○ slim

25 Which word BEST completes the
sentence below?

They _____ in the van to go.

○ camp

○ dump

○ jump

Writing to Inform

Read the prompt and plan your response.

Most people have an animal they like best.

Think about an animal you like best.

Write a description of your animal. Then draw a picture to go with your description.

Planning Page

Use this space to make notes before you start writing. The writing on this page will NOT be scored.

_____

- - - - - - - - - - - - - - - - - - -

_____

_____

- - - - - - - - - - - - - - - - - - -

_____

Read Together To the teacher: Read this page with children. Have them plan their writing on this page. Direct them to write their description on the following page. Then have them draw their picture in the box.

Name _____ Date _____

Start your response here. The writing on this page and the drawing on the next page WILL be scored.

_____

- -

_____

_____

- -

_____

_____

- -

_____

_____

- -

_____

_____

- -

_____

_____

- -

_____

Name _____ Date _____

Reading and Analyzing Text

Read the stories "Jill's New Cat" and "A Dog Walk" before answering Numbers 1 through 8.

Jill's New Cat

Jill felt glad. She would get a cat.

Dad and Jill went to a place that had lots of animals. The animals did not have a place to live. Jill and Dad went to see the cats.

A big white cat bumped Jill's leg. It had two blue eyes. Jill bent down and picked it up. The cat was soft.

Name _____ Date _____

"This is my cat," Jill said. "She will be a good friend for me."

"Do you see the little cat?" asked Dad. "A little cat will run and play with you."

"No, I picked the best cat," said Jill. "I will call her Puff."

Dad looked at the smile on Jill's face. He nodded. Puff would have a good place to live.

A Dog Walk

Ben got up. He had to walk his brown dog Jo-Jo. Ben got his shoes and put them on. Then Ben headed for the door. Jo-Jo heard his footsteps. Jo-Jo ran to the door! Jo-Jo jumped up and down. She looked at Ben. Then she looked at the door. Jo-Jo did this many times.

"Good morning, Jo-Jo," Ben said. "Are you ready for a walk? It looks like a sunny day. Let's go!"

Jo-Jo walked with Ben. They stopped at the mailbox. Jo-Jo wanted to sit. They stopped at the street. Jo-Jo wanted to bark. They stopped at the grass. Jo-Jo wanted to roll in it. They stopped at the tree. Jo-Jo wanted to dig.

Ben bent down to Jo-Jo. He looked her in the eyes. "You are a silly brown dog," Ben said with a smile. "Maybe we can try to walk tomorrow." Jo-Jo licked Ben on the face.

Now answer Numbers 1 through 8. Base your answers on the stories "Jill's New Cat" and "A Dog Walk."

1 Read this sentence from the story "Jill's New Cat."

Jill bent down and picked it up.

What does the word *down* mean in the sentence above?

○ not up

○ in here

○ too soft

2 Read this sentence from the story "Jill's New Cat."

"A little cat will run and play with you."

What does the word *play* mean in the sentence above?

○ grow

○ rest

○ have fun

Name _____   Date _____

3 What happens AFTER Jill names the cat in
the story "Jill's New Cat"?

○ Dad nods.

○ The cat naps.

○ Jill picks up the cat.

4 Read this sentence from the story
"A Dog Walk."

He had to walk his brown dog Jo-Jo.

Which word is a color word in the sentence above?

○ walk

○ brown

○ dog

5 How does Jo-Jo know Ben is ready for their
walk in the story "A Dog Walk"?

○ He sees Ben at the door.

○ He hears Ben's footsteps.

○ He knows that it is a nice day.

6 Read this sentence from the story
"A Dog Walk."

Ben bent down to Jo-Jo.

What does the word *bent* mean in the
sentence above?

○ pick up

○ lean over

○ sit next to

7 How are Jill and Ben ALIKE?

○ They like their pets.

○ They walk their pets.

○ They find their pets.

8 What is true about the pets in
BOTH stories?

○ Both pets are white.

○ Both pets have new friends.

○ Both pets have good homes.

Read the article "What Lives in a Pond?" before answering Numbers 9 through 15.

What Lives in a Pond?

A pond is a place filled with water. Plants and animals both live in a pond.

A fish is an animal. It has fins that flap. It has skin made of scales. The scales are flat. The fins and scales help the fish swim.

Name _____ Date _____

A frog is an animal. It can live in water. It can live on the land, too. It has four legs. The two back legs are long. The back legs help the frog swim in water. They help the frog hop on land.

Grass is a plant. It grows in the mud of the pond. Fish and frogs swim into the grass. The grass helps them hide. Big animals cannot see them. Then the big animals cannot eat the fish and frogs.

Now answer Numbers 9 through 15. Base your answers on the article "What Lives in a Pond?"

9 Read this sentence from the article.

A pond is a place filled with water.

Which picture shows what the word *water* means in the sentence above?

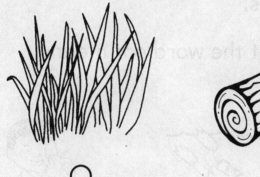  

○ ○ ○

10 Read this sentence from the article.

It has fins that flap.

Which word means almost the SAME as the word *flap* in the sentence above?

○ stop

○ take

○ wave

Name _____ Date _____

11 What helps fish swim?

○ legs and fins

○ fins and scales

○ scales and legs

12 Read this sentence from the article.

**Then the big animals cannot
eat the fish and frogs.**

Which picture shows what the word *eat* means
in the sentence above?

  ○

13 Which caption BEST tells about the LAST picture in the article?

○ What Fish Look Like

○ How the Frog Hides

○ When the Frog Hops

14 What is the MAIN idea of the article?

○ "Fish and frogs swim into the grass."

○ "Plants and animals both live in a pond."

○ "The back legs help the frog swim in water."

15 Why did the author write the article?

○ to tell a fun tale

○ to tell what lives in a pond

○ to get you to hike to a pond

Name _____ Date _____

Phonics

Answer Numbers 16 through 25. Choose the best answer for each question.

16 Which word BEST completes the sentence below?

Jake's dog had to get a _____.

○ back

○ batch

○ bath

17 Which word BEST completes the sentence below?

The dog _____ like water.

○ aren't

○ didn't

○ isn't

 Read Together To the teacher: Read the directions and questions with children. Target sentences and answer choices should be read independently.

18 Which word BEST completes the sentence below?

Jake had to _____ the dog.

○ cash

○ cast

○ catch

19 Which word BEST completes the sentence below?

The dog went into the _____ .

○ tab

○ top

○ tub

20 Which word BEST completes the sentence below?

_____ all wet now!

○ He's

○ Let's

○ Aren't

47

Name _____ Date _____

21 Which word BEST completes the sentence below?

The dog starts to _____.

- ○ fine
- ○ slime
- ○ whine

22 Which word BEST completes the sentence below?

Watch out! The dog is going to _____.

- ○ shake
- ○ shine
- ○ shop

23 Which word BEST completes the sentence below?

Did you see the water _____ on Jake?

- ○ flash
- ○ scratch
- ○ splash

24 Which word BEST completes the

sentence below?

Look at the water _____ off Jake.

○ clip

○ dip

○ drip

25 Which word BEST completes the

sentence below?

Jake and the dog are both _____!

○ wet

○ win

○ wit

Writing to Inform

Read the prompt and plan your response.

Most people have a favorite snack.
Think about a snack you like.
Now write about how to make your favorite snack.

Planning Page

Use this space to make notes before you start writing. The writing on this page will NOT be scored.

_____

- -

_____

_____

- -

_____

To the teacher: Read this page with children. Have them plan their writing on this page. Direct them to write their response on the following two pages.

Start your response here. The writing on this page and the next page WILL be scored.

_____

- -

_____

_____

- -

_____

_____

- -

_____

_____

- -

_____

_____

- -

_____

_____

- -

_____

Name _____ Date _____

Reading and Analyzing Text

Read the story "The Box" before answering Numbers 1 through 8.

The Box

It is raining. Jess and Beth stay inside. They look for some things to do.

Jess and Beth find an old box. They walk around it. They want to know what is inside the box.

Jess and Beth carry the box to their mother. Mom opens it. The box holds old things.

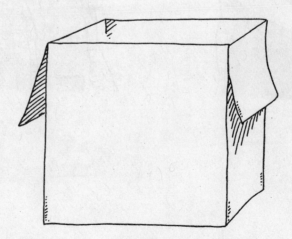

 To the teacher: Read the directions and questions with children. Selection and answer choices should be read independently.

Name _____ Date _____

"I played with these when I was little," Mom tells Jess and Beth.

Jess likes the boat. Beth likes the car.

Mom picks up a small box. It is gray. She lifts the top. The box plays a sweet tune.

Name _____ Date _____

Now answer Numbers 1 through 8. Base your answers on the story "The Box."

1 Why are Jess and Beth inside?

    ⭘ It is raining.

    ⭘ They are sick.

    ⭘ They must help Mom clean.

2 Read this sentence from the story.

    Jess and Beth find an old box.

What does the word *old* mean in the sentence above?

    ⭘ not new

    ⭘ too soft

    ⭘ very funny

3 Read this sentence from the story.

**Jess and Beth carry the box
to their mother.**

What does the word *carry* mean in the
sentence above?

○ like

○ sing

○ take

4 What happens AFTER Jess and Beth take
the box to Mom?

○ Mom opens the box.

○ Mom puts the box away.

○ Mom puts things in the box.

5 How are Jess and Beth ALIKE?

○ They both stay inside.

○ They both like the rain.

○ They both open the box.

6 How are the boat and the car the SAME?

○ They both have wheels.

○ Mom played with them both.

○ They both play a sweet tune.

7 Read this sentence from the story.

Mom picks up a small box.

Which word means almost the SAME as the word *small* in the sentence above?

○ big

○ brown

○ little

8 Read this sentence from the story.

The box plays a sweet tune.

What does the word *plays* mean in the sentence above?

○ has fun

○ makes a song

○ acts on a stage

Name _____ Date _____

Read the article "A Note for You" before answering Numbers 9 through 15.

A Note for You

A friend writes on paper. It is a note for you. She puts it in a mailbox. How do you get it?

First, someone gets the note. It goes in a bag. Then it goes to a mail place.

Next, someone looks at the zip code. The zip code tells where you live. Mail with the same zip code goes in one box.

A truck picks up the box. It drives to a mail place by you.

Someone reads your name and your street. She will bring the note to you.

Now answer Numbers 9 through 15. Base your answers on the article "A Note for You."

9 What is the MAIN idea of the article?

○ Trucks bring the mail.

○ Mail is put inside bags.

○ You see how mail gets to you.

10 Read this sentence from the article.

She puts it in a mailbox.

What does the word *mailbox* mean in the sentence above?

○ a box on a truck

○ a box to put mail in

○ a box to send as a gift

Name _____ Date _____

11 What is a zip code?

○ the name of a street

○ a code for where someone lives

○ a fast truck that drives the mail

12 Read this sentence from the article.

A truck picks up the box.

What is a *truck*?

○ something to ride in

○ a person who brings mail

○ a big box to put your note in

13 Read this sentence from the article.

She will bring the note to you.

What does the word *bring* mean in the sentence above?

○ lots of mail

○ take to a new place

○ someone who sends mail

Name _____ Date _____

14 Why is a name put on mail?

○ to tell who it is for

○ to tell who will drive the truck

○ to tell who will put it in a mail bag

15 Why did the author write this article?

○ to tell a funny story

○ to get you to send mail

○ to tell things about mail

STOP

Name _____ Date _____

Phonics

Answer Numbers 16 through 25. Choose the best answer for each question.

16 Which word BEST completes the sentence below?

Steve and Jay had a _____.

○ into

○ under

○ sleepover

17 Which word BEST completes the sentence below?

The _____ came down.

○ rain

○ rent

○ run

18 Which word BEST completes the sentence below?

   "Let's play hide and _____," said Jay.

   ○ sack

   ○ seek

   ○ sick

19 Which word BEST completes the sentence below?

   "I will _____ my eyes first," he said.

   ○ case

   ○ class

   ○ close

20 Which word BEST completes the sentence below?

Steve ran up the steps and saw a _____ pile of quilts.

○ hug

○ huge

○ hung

21 Which word BEST completes the sentence below?

Steve said, "Look at all _____ quilts!"

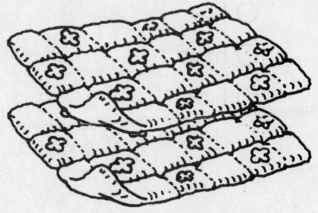

○ teach

○ then

○ these

22 Which word BEST completes the sentence below?

"_____ hide under them," he said.

- ○ I'll
- ○ Isn't
- ○ It's

23 Which word BEST completes the sentence below?

Steve pulled the quilts over his _____.

- ○ hay
- ○ head
- ○ hide

Name _____ Date _____

24 Which word BEST completes the sentence below?

"I give up!" Jay _____. "Where are you?"

○ grand

○ groaned

○ grow

25 Which word BEST completes the sentence below?

"_____ good at this game!" he said.

○ You'll

○ You're

○ You've

Name _____ Date _____

Revising and Editing

Answer Numbers 1 through 10. Choose the best answer for each question.

1 Which word is spelled WRONG in the sentence below?

Lee sat under a tri.

○ sat

○ under

○ tri

2 Which word should begin with a capital letter in the sentence below?

Soon it would be mother's Day.

○ it

○ would

○ mother's

3 Which punctuation mark should END the sentence below?

What gift would Lee get for Mom

○ .

○ ?

○ !

4 What is the CORRECT way to write the date in the sentence below?

Lee gave his mom a gift on May 10 2009.

○ May 10, 2009

○ May, 10 2009

○ May 10 2009,

5 Which word is WRONG in the sentence below?

She opened it under lunch.

○ opened

○ under

○ lunch

6 What change could be made in the sentences below?

It was a mug. She liked it.

○ It was a mug she liked it.

○ It was a mug but she like it.

○ It was a mug, and she liked it.

7 Which word is WRONG in the sentence below?

"I know what I will gives Mom this time," Lee said.

○ know

○ gives

○ time

8 Which word is WRONG in the sentence below?

"I am go to get her some plant seeds."

○ go

○ some

○ seeds

9 Which word is spelled WRONG in the sentence below?

"Mom likes to grai plants," Lee said.

○ likes

○ grai

○ plants

10 Which word is WRONG in the sentence below?

I can buy seeds on the store.

○ I

○ on

○ store

Writing to Narrate

Read the prompt and plan your response.

> Most people have had a problem.
>
> Think about a problem you have had and how you solved it.
>
> Now write about your problem and how you solved it.

Planning Page

Use this space to make notes before you start writing. The writing on this page will NOT be scored.

_____

- - - - - - - - - - - - - - - - - - -

_____

- - - - - - - - - - - - - - - - - - -

_____

 To the teacher: Read this page with children. Have them plan their writing on this page. Direct them to write their response on the following two pages.

Unit Test, Writing to Narrate   72   Grade 1, Unit 4
© Houghton Mifflin Harcourt Publishing Company. All rights reserved.

Name _____ Date _____

Start your response here. The writing on this page and the next page WILL be scored.

_____

- -

_____

- -

_____

_____

- -

_____

- -

_____

- -

_____

_____

- -

_____

Name _____ Date _____

Name _____ Date _____

Reading Complex Text

Read the story "Little Wolf's Lesson." As you read, stop and answer each question. Use examples from the story to support your answers.

Little Wolf's Lesson

Little Wolf lived under the trees with Great Wolf. Great Wolf's job was to show Little Wolf how to see, hear, and smell like a wolf. Then Little Wolf could grow up to be a great wolf.

 To the teacher: Read the directions and questions with children. Selection should be read independently.

"First you must see," Great Wolf said. "With your eyes, you can see the blue sky and the green grass. Your eyes seeing will make you a good wolf. Tell me what you see."

Little Wolf looked around. "I see a snake under a plant. I see a leaf fall from a tree."

---

❶ Who is telling this story?

_____

_____

_____

_____

"Next you must hear," Great Wolf said. "With your hearing, you can tell where the animals are. You can hear the birds with their songs. You can hear the sheep go BAA! Your hearing will make you a good wolf. Tell me what you hear."

Name _____ Date _____

Little Wolf sat still. Then he said, "I hear the crow go CAW! I hear the bees go BUZZ!"

---

2 What words from the story show what Little Wolf can hear?

_____

- -

_____

_____

- -

_____

_____

- -

_____

"There is one more lesson. It will make you a great wolf," Great Wolf said. "You have the gift of smelling. You can smell things that are far away."

Little Wolf said, "How can smelling make me a great wolf? I am sure that seeing and hearing will make me a great wolf first. I don't need to use my smelling."

Name _____ Date _____

When Great Wolf was little, he felt just like Little Wolf. "Please hear me, Little Wolf," Great Wolf said. "Your gift of smelling is the best skill you have. It lets you see what cannot be seen."

Little Wolf felt lost. "But I can see and hear all that I need to," he said.

3 Why does Little Wolf feel lost?

_____

- -

_____

- -

_____

- -

_____

"Look at the wind. Tell me what you see," said Great Wolf.

Little Wolf looked up and said, "I cannot see the wind."

Great Wolf said, "Close your eyes. Smell the wind. Then tell me what you see." Little Wolf closed his eyes.

He smelled the wind. Then he saw many things. With his eyes closed, he could see Bird and Turtle. He knew they were close, but he could not see or hear them. He could smell the water of a stream, but he could not see or hear it.

Little Wolf was glad. He opened his eyes and saw Great Wolf looking at him. Little Wolf said, "We *can* see what cannot be seen. Smell will make me a great wolf."

4 Name one thing Little Wolf saw when he closed his eyes. What lesson does he learn from this?

_____

_____

_____

_____

Reading and Analyzing Text

**Read the story "What a Kite!" before answering
Numbers 1 through 8.**

What a Kite!

The Young family went to the park. They took a lunch.
While eating, Carl and Joy watched some girls and boys
fly kites.

"I wish we had a kite," said Joy. "It would be fun to
fly it."

"We'll come to the park again," said Joy's mother.
"Then we will bring a kite."

"Wait!" said Carl. "I know what we can do."

To the teacher: Read the directions and questions with children. Selection and answer choices should be
read independently.

Carl ran to the car. He got some yarn that was in his mother's bag. Then he got their lunch bag. Carl fixed the yarn to the open end of the bag.

"Here, Joy," Carl said. "Run with the yarn to make the bag fly." In no time, Joy had the kite flying.

Joy said, "It may not be a real kite, but it is still fun."

And it was.

Now answer Numbers 1 through 8. Base your answers on the story "What a Kite!"

1 What is Joy's MAIN problem in this story?

○ She wants a kite.

○ She wants to eat lunch.

○ She wants to run with Jake.

2 Read this sentence from the story.

"I know what we can do."

What does the word *know* mean in the sentence above?

○ have a plan

○ see a friend

○ like to make

3 Read this sentence from the story.

Carl ran to the car.

What does the word *car* mean in the sentence above?

○ a playground

○ a tray that holds food

○ a ride that has wheels

4 What happens AFTER Carl gets some yarn?

○ The family eats lunch.

○ Carl gets the lunch bag.

○ Joy watches boys and girls fly kites.

5 Read this sentence from the story.

Carl fixed the yarn to the open end of the bag.

Which word is an action word in the sentence above?

○ fixed

○ the

○ yarn

Name _____ Date _____

6 What happens AFTER Carl gives Joy the bag fixed with yarn?

○ Joy blows on it.

○ Joy runs with it.

○ Joy puts it in the car.

7 Read this sentence from the story.

It may not be a real kite, but it is still fun.

Which word means almost the SAME as the word *real* in the sentence above?

○ fake

○ new

○ true

8 How does Joy feel at the END of the story?

○ glad

○ mad

○ sad

Read the articles "Ants" and "The Red Fox" before answering Numbers 9 through 15.

Ants

Ants live in many places. They are very small. Ants live in a big family. An ant family lives in a nest. Ant nests can be in the ground or on top of the ground. Some ants make nests in trees.

Ants have jobs to do. Each ant does one job, but the ants work together like a team. One ant is the queen. Just one queen lives in a nest. The queen lays eggs. That is her main job.

Some ants clean the nest. Some ants look for food, like seeds. They bring the food back to the nest. One group of ants feeds baby ants. All the ants work hard. It helps the family grow.

The Red Fox

The red fox looks like a small dog. It has long legs which help it run fast. The red fox goes in many places. It likes grass, farms, and trees. It has been seen where people live, too. The red fox lives in a place called a den.

If the red fox is a girl, called a female, she might have a baby fox. A fox baby is a pup. But she wouldn't have just one pup in her den. The female red fox can have 3 to 12 pups a year!

Name _____ Date _____

The red fox eats a lot. It eats many foods. It eats bugs and berries. It eats scraps left over by people. The red fox hunts, too. It hunts in the day. It hunts when it is dark out. It has good eyes and ears to hunt when it is dark. It can see and hear a small animal, like a mouse.

**Now answer Numbers 9 through 15. Base
your answers on the articles "Ants" and
"The Red Fox."**

9 What does the title tell you the article
"Ants" will be about?

   ○ It will tell about ants.

   ○ It will tell about queens.

   ○ It will tell about a family.

10 Read this sentence from the article "Ants."

**Ant nests can be in the ground
or on top of the ground.**

What does the word *top* mean in the
sentence above?

   ○ a shirt

   ○ a toy that spins

   ○ the part that is up

11 What is the MAIN idea of the article "Ants"?

○ An ant family lives in a nest.

○ Ants have jobs that help their family.

○ Some ants look for food to bring to the nest.

12 Read this sentence from the article
"The Red Fox."

It has been seen where people live, too.

What does the word *where* mean in the
sentence above?

○ at a time

○ on top of

○ in a place

13 Read this sentence from the article "The Red Fox."

A fox baby is a pup.

What does the word *baby* mean in the sentence above?

○ an old animal

○ a place to sleep

○ a very young animal

14 What are BOTH articles MOSTLY about?

○ animals

○ jobs

○ seasons

15 How is the home of ants DIFFERENT from the home of a red fox?

○ Ants live in nests. A red fox lives in a den.

○ Ants live with people. A red fox lives in a nest.

○ Ants live in dens. A red fox lives in the ground.

Name _____ Date _____

Phonics

Answer Numbers 16 through 25. Choose the best answer for each question.

16 Which word BEST completes the sentence below?

> **Can a rock be a funny pet? Follow these _____ to make a pet rock.**

- ○ steps
- ○ steep
- ○ stops

17 Which word BEST completes the sentence below?

> **First, you will _____ to find a rock.**

- ○ nail
- ○ need
- ○ nod

 Read Together To the teacher: Read the directions and questions with children. Target sentences and answer choices should be read independently.

18 Which word BEST completes the sentence below?

Look for one _____ is small and round.

○ chat

○ hat

○ that

19 Which word BEST completes the sentence below?

The rock should be _____, too.

○ smell

○ smith

○ smooth

20 Which word BEST completes the sentence below?

Next, wash the _____ off.

○ sail

○ seal

○ soil

21 Which word BEST completes the sentence below?

Then, pick a _____ or zoo animal to make.

○ farm

○ firm

○ foam

22 Which word BEST completes the sentence below?

Now _____ the parts on the animal.

○ paint

○ pant

○ point

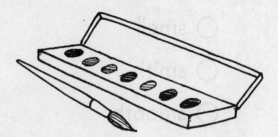

23 Which word BEST completes the sentence below?

You can add things like the _____, paws, and tail.

○ face

○ fast

○ fuss

Name _____ Date _____

24 Which word BEST completes the sentence below?

Set the rock on paper until the paint _____ wet.

○ I'm

○ isn't

○ it's

25 Which word BEST completes the sentence below?

It will not be _____ before you have a pet rock!

○ lone

○ long

○ lost

Revising and Editing

Answer Numbers 1 through 10. Choose the best answer for each question.

1 Which word BEST completes the sentence below?

Next week, my family _____ sell some things.

○ had

○ was

○ will

2 Which word BEST completes the sentence below?

_____ looked for things to sell.

○ Mom and I

○ I and Mom

○ Mom and me

To the teacher: Read the directions and questions with children. Target sentences and answer choices should be read independently.

3 Which word is spelled WRONG in the sentence below?

My dod helped, too.

○ dod

○ helped

○ too

4 Which word BEST completes the sentence below?

I _____ find many things to sell.

○ can't

○ isn't

○ weren't

5 Which word describes the dishes in the sentence below?

Mom pulled out some blue dishes.

○ blue

○ out

○ pulled

6 Which word BEST completes the sentence below?

> **The dishes _____ a gift.**

○ is

○ was

○ were

7 Which word BEST completes the sentence below?

> **One of _____ friends gave the dishes to us.**

○ her

○ hers

○ she

8 Which word is WRONG in the sentence below?

> **Then we looked at all of my toy.**

○ looked

○ my

○ toy

9 Which word BEST completes the sentence below?

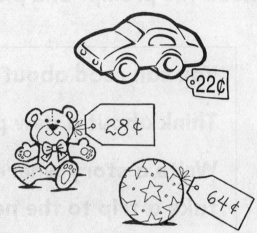

I am _____ to sell the ones I don't like.

○ go

○ going

○ will

10 Which word is spelled WRONG in the sentence below?

Now my toy box will nat be so full.

○ nat

○ so

○ will

Writing to Narrate

Read the prompt and plan your response.

You can read about new places in stories.

Think about a new place you have read about.

Write a story where you pretend to
take a trip to the new place.

Planning Page

Use this space to make notes before you start
writing. The writing on this page will NOT be
scored.

_____

- -

_____

_____

- -

_____

 To the teacher: Read this page with children. Have them plan their writing on this page. Direct them to write their
response on the following two pages.

Name _____ Date _____

Start your response here. The writing on this page and the next page WILL be scored.

Name _____ Date _____

Start your response here. The writing on this
page and the next page will be scored.

Reading Complex Text

Read the articles "Are All Elephants the Same?" and "How Does an Elephant's Body Work?" As you read, stop and answer each question. Use examples from the articles to support your answers.

Are All Elephants the Same?

You can see elephants at the zoo. You can see them around the world, too! Are all elephants the same? How can you tell?

African Elephants

Some elephants live in Africa. They are called African elephants. They live mostly in woods and on plains.

African elephants are the biggest land animals on Earth. They have big ears, too. African elephants use their ears to cover up and stay cool in the heat. They also cool off with their trunks. They suck water up into their trunks and give themselves a shower.

African elephants also have tusks. Tusks are big teeth. Both males and females have tusks. They use their tusks to dig for food and water.

To the teacher: Read the directions and questions with children. Before children read the passage, explain the terms African, Africa, Asian, and Asia. Passage should be read independently.

Name _____ Date _____

1 How do African elephants use their ears?

_____

- -

_____

- -

_____

- -

_____

- -

_____

Asian Elephants

Some elephants live in Asia. They are called Asian elephants. They live on land that has grass, plants, and trees.

Asian elephants are big, but they are smaller than African elephants. They have smaller ears, too. They move their ears a lot. This helps them stay cool in the heat. Asian elephants also take showers with their trunks.

Not all Asian elephants have tusks, only some of the males do. Like African elephants, they use their tusks to find food and water.

Name _____ Date _____

More About Elephants

Which elephant?	Where do they live?	About how long do they live?	About how tall do they grow?
African elephant	Africa	70 years	8 to 13 feet
Asian elephant	Asia	60 years	6 to 10 feet

2 About how long does the Asian elephant live?

_____

_ _

_____

_ _

_____

_ _

_____

How Does an Elephant's Body Work?

How do elephants drink? How do they get food without hands? How do they move around? The parts of an elephant's body have important uses.

Trunks

Elephants use their trunks in many ways. They breathe with their trunks. In fact, they use their trunks more than their mouths to breathe. Elephants drink with their trunks, too. They draw water up into their trunks. Then they spray the water in their mouths. Elephants use their trunks like fingers, too. They can grab food. Elephants are skilled with their trunks. They can even take the shells off of small peanuts!

❸ How is an elephant's trunk like fingers?

_____

- - - - - - - - - - - - - - - - - -

_____

_____

- - - - - - - - - - - - - - - - - -

_____

_____

Tusks

Elephant tusks are very big teeth. They are long and can be sharp at the ends. Most elephants have tusks, but some don't. Elephants use their tusks to move things. They move trees and bushes out of their way. They also use their tusks to dig to find water and food.

Legs

An elephant's legs are long, big, and strong. They use their legs to walk up and down hills. They also use them to swim in deep water. Because elephants are so big, they have soft pads on their feet. The pads help their legs stay strong.

Name _____ Date _____

4 What do BOTH articles say about an
elephant's tusks?

_____

- -

_____

- -

_____

_____

- -

_____

Reading and Analyzing Text

**Read the story "The Boat Ride" before answering
Numbers 1 through 8.**

The Boat Ride

Fred Frog lived in a pond. He loved to swim in the cold water.

One day Bud Bird came to see Fred.

"Hi, Bud!" Fred called out. "It is a nice day!"

"Yes, it is," said Bud. "But it is a little hot. I wish I could play on the water like you."

Fred didn't want Bud to be unhappy. He had an idea!

 To the teacher: Read the directions and questions with children. Selection and answer choices should be read independently.

Name _____ Date _____

Fred swam to some plants. He got the biggest one. He quickly pushed it near Bud. Bud hopped on. The leaf was a boat.

"This is not too hard to do. This is a breeze!" cried Bud. "Thank you, Fred!"

Name _____ Date _____

Now answer Numbers 1 through 8. Base your answers on the story "The Boat Ride."

1 Where does the story take place?

   ○ at a park

   ○ at a pond

   ○ at a school

2 Read this sentence from the story.

He loved to swim in the cold water.

What does the word *loved* mean in the sentence above?

   ○ did not like

   ○ liked a lot

   ○ liked a little

3 When does the story take place?

   ○ on a cold day

   ○ on a rainy day

   ○ on a sunny day

4 How is Fred DIFFERENT from Bud?

○ Fred can fly.

○ Fred can swim.

○ Fred eats bugs.

5 Read this sentence from the story.

Fred didn't want Bud to be unhappy.

Which word group BEST fits the way the word
unhappy is used in the sentence above?

○ family

○ feelings

○ time

6 Read this sentence from the story.

He quickly pushed it near Bud.

What does the word *near* mean in the
sentence above?

○ out of

○ close to

○ far away

Name _____ Date _____

7 Read these sentences from the story.

> **"This is not too hard to do. This
> is a breeze!" cried Bud.**

What does *this is a breeze* mean in the

sentence above?

○ It is easy.

○ It is windy.

○ It feels cold.

8 Read the chart below.

How Bud Feels	
At Start of Story	**At End of Story**
upset	

How does Bud feel at the END of the story?

○ sad

○ mad

○ glad

Name _____ Date _____

Read the article "A Sailboat Needs Wind" before answering Numbers 9 through 15.

A Sailboat Needs Wind

You can ride in a sailboat. It will take you across the water. A sailboat is unlike most boats. It does not use gas to make it go. It uses wind!

A sailboat has a large sail. It is made of cloth. People lift the sail high on a pole.

Wind pushes things. For sailing, it should be blowing in the back of the boat. Wind fills the sail. The cloth blocks the wind. The wind keeps pushing on the sail. It makes the boat go.

A strong wind makes the boat go faster. If the wind stops, the boat will stop, too.

Name _____ Date _____

Now answer Numbers 9 through 15. Base your answers on the article "A Sailboat Needs Wind."

9 What is this article MOSTLY about?

○ sailing

○ strong wind

○ sewing cloth

10 Read this sentence from the article.

You can ride in a sailboat.

What does the word *ride* mean in the sentence above?

○ get in and go

○ something at a park

○ to throw something away

11 Read this sentence from the article.

A sailboat is unlike most boats.

What does the word *unlike* mean in the sentence above?

○ not like

○ just like

○ like again

12 How are sailboats DIFFERENT from most boats?

○ They use gas to go.

○ They use wind to go.

○ You cannot ride in them.

13 Read this sentence from the article.

A sailboat has a large sail.

What does the word *large* mean in the sentence above?

○ big

○ many

○ white

Name _____ Date _____

14 How do you know this article is true?

○ It tells facts.

○ It tells a story.

○ It tells about boats.

15 Read this sentence from the article.

The cloth blocks the wind.

What does the word *blocks* mean in the

sentence above?

○ fills

○ makes

○ stops

STOP

Name _____ Date _____

Phonics

Answer Numbers 16 through 25. Choose the best answer for each question.

16 Which word BEST completes the sentence below?

The sun's _____ woke Jean.

○ late

○ light

○ list

17 Which word BEST completes the sentence below?

She _____ out of bed.

○ hoped

○ hopped

○ hot

To the teacher: Read the directions and questions with children. Target sentences and answer choices should be read independently.

18 Which word BEST completes the sentence below?

She got dressed _____.

○ quickly

○ quite

○ quiz

19 Which word BEST completes the sentence below?

Jean was feeling _____.

○ happen

○ happy

○ hay

20 Which word BEST completes the sentence below?

She was going to a horse _____.

○ stable

○ stacking

○ stamps

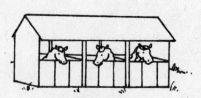

21 Which word BEST completes the sentence below?

She was not going to be _____.

○ she

○ shine

○ shy

22 Which word BEST completes the sentence below?

Jean would ask for the _____ horse.

○ nicest

○ niciest

○ nicyest

23 Which word BEST completes the sentence below?

She did not want to be _____.

○ unsafe

○ unsay

○ untie

24 Which word BEST completes the sentence below?

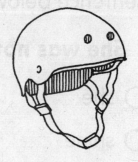

She packed a helmet _____ she could put it on her head.

○ say

○ see

○ so

25 Which word BEST completes the sentence below?

It was in her _____ backpack.

○ pears

○ purple

○ pull

STOP

Name _____ Date _____

Revising and Editing

Answer Numbers 1 through 10. Choose the best answer for each question.

1 Which word is spelled WRONG in the sentence below?

Gail wanted to make a pai.

○ make

○ pai

○ wanted

2 Which word is spelled WRONG in the sentence below?

She looked at the peaches on the tawble.

○ looked

○ peaches

○ tawble

Read Together To the teacher: Read the directions and questions with children. Target sentences and answer choices should be read independently.

3 Which word BEST completes the sentence below?

The fuzzy peaches had a _____ smell.

- ○ bumpy
- ○ loud
- ○ sweet

4 Which punctuation mark should END the sentence below?

Could Gail use them to bake a good treat

- ○ .
- ○ ?
- ○ !

5 Which word BEST completes the sentence below?

Gail picked up the _____ peach of all.

- ○ big
- ○ bigger
- ○ biggest

6 Which word tells how the peach felt in the sentence below?

The peach was too hard.

○ hard

○ too

○ was

7 Which word BEST completes the sentence below?

"Come try the plums over _____," said Ron.

○ here

○ this

○ when

8 Which punctuation mark should END the sentence below?

Gail took a bite of a plum

○ .

○ ?

○ ,

9 Which word BEST completes the sentence below?

The plum was _____ good.

○ soft

○ very

○ walk

10 Which punctuation mark should END the sentence below?

These plums are yummy

○ ,

○ ?

○ !

Writing Opinions

Read the story "Earth Day" before responding to the prompt.

Earth Day

Ann walked into school. She saw big pictures on the walls. Some of the pictures were of trees. Some showed paper and cans. Other pictures were of bikes and plants. One picture had big letters on it. "SAVE THE EARTH!" Now Ann got it. It was Earth Day.

Ann went to her class. Miss Long was there. "Good morning, class," Miss Long said. "Today is Earth Day. What can we do to help our earth? It is a *big* job! I want you to list some ways we can help."

Ann's classmates were writing. Ann didn't. She could not think of a way to help. Ann looked sad. Miss Long stopped at her desk. "Ann, can I help you?" she asked.

"Miss Long, I can't think of even one big thing," Ann said. "I ride my bike to school. I put our cans in a

Read Together To the teacher: Read the directions with children. Selection should be read independently. Then read the next page and have children plan their writing. Direct them to write their responses on the following two pages.

Unit Test, Writing Opinions
127
Grade 1, Unit 6

bag. I planted a tree last spring. But these are small things," Ann said with a frown.

"Oh, Ann! Small things are just as good as big things!"

Now respond to the prompt. Base your response on the story "Earth Day."

In "Earth Day," Miss Long says, "Small things are just as good as big things!"

Think about whether or not you feel the SAME way.

Write a response that tells why or why not.

Planning Page

Use this space to make notes before you start writing. The writing on this page will NOT be scored.

_____
- - - - - - - - - - - - - - - - - -
_____
- - - - - - - - - - - - - - - - - -
_____
- - - - - - - - - - - - - - - - - -
_____

Name _____ Date _____

Start your response here. The writing on this page and the next page WILL be scored.

_____

- -

_____

_____

- -

_____

_____

- -

_____

_____

- -

_____

_____

- -

_____

_____

- -

_____

Name _____ Date _____

Reading Complex Text

Read the poem "The Counting Lesson" and the story "A Family Tree." As you read, stop and answer each question. Use examples from the poem and the story to support your answers.

The Counting Lesson

by Emilie Poulsson

Here is the beehive. Where are the bees?

Hidden away where nobody sees.

Soon they come creeping out of the hive—

One!—two!—three! four! *five!*

To the teacher: Read the directions and questions with children. Passage should be read independently.

Once I saw an ant hill

With no ants about;

So I said, "Dear little ants,

Won't you please come out?"

Then as if the little ants

Had heard my call—

One! two! three! four! *five* came out!

And that was all!

---

1 Why can the narrator NOT see the bees at the START of the poem?

_____

- -

_____

_____

_____

- -

_____

_____

- -

_____

Name _____ Date _____

A Family Tree

In our yard, we have a big tree. In the tree, I can see a nest. I want to see what is inside the nest. I know from school that different animals live in nests. Many of these animals are birds. I don't see any birds at all. The nest is up too high for me to see inside it. I wonder how I might get a better look.

❷ What is the narrator's problem in this story?

_____

_____

_____

_____

The nest looks like it is made of grass. The grass looks like it is held together with mud. It is mostly brown and green.

Name _____ Date _____

I ask Dad what he thinks might be in there. He thinks a mother bird laid pretty blue eggs in the nest. Mom tells me these birds are called robins. She says that the babies hatch from the eggs. Then they wait for their mother to feed them. Mom says I should leave them alone. Their mother needs to feed and care for them. But I sure want to take a look.

Climbing the tree is not a good idea. I might upset the nest. I go to the window in my bedroom. I am high enough to see the nest, but it is too far away. I can't see the birds.

❸ Why does the narrator say climbing the tree is NOT a good idea?

_____
- -
_____
_____
- -
_____
_____

Wait, I have a great idea! In the closet, I find a pair of binoculars. These are like strong eyeglasses you look through. Binoculars make something far away look close. I take them with me to the window.

I can see the baby birds now. There they are—one, two, three, four, five! They are small and brown. Their mouths stay open for a long time.

I can see right inside the little nest. I won't even bother them one bit.

❹ How is the narrator of the poem the SAME as the narrator of the story?

_____

- -

_____

_____

- -

_____

_____

- -

_____